Y0-DKB-674

The Happiness Mindset:

12 Strategies for Happiness & Success I Wish Someone Had Told Me When I Was Young

By Brandon Stanberg

Introduction

Life can be challenging. It can be scary or sad and sometimes it can just be a chore. Life can also be beautiful, exciting and rewarding. It is a cycle of highs and lows. No one escapes this cycle. My goal in writing this book is to ensure your life is tipped in favour of one that is amazing, inspiring and filled with happiness and success.

The strategies outlined in this book will change your approach to life and empower you to employ a 'winning' mindset at all times. These strategies are based on my own lessons learned as a result of negative relationships that were not right for me, a career that was never my passion, poor health and chronic stress. Whilst at the time these were painful experiences, they taught me invaluable lessons on how you can re-build your life from a place of negativity to a life of resilience, success and ultimately happiness. The 12 strategies I share here will change your life for the better. They will put you back in the driving seat so that you can drive your life forward in the direction you want; and empower you to choose a life filled with happiness and achievement.

You can read different chapters at different times without necessarily having to trawl through each chapter in turn. I guarantee you will find value in each and every strategy; if you employ these strategies, your life will never be the same again.

Table of Contents

Strategy 1: Self-motivation, Self-worth, Self-respect, Self-care & Ultimately a Self-purpose

"Your time is limited, so don't waste it living someone else's life. Don't be trapped by dogma — which is living with the results of other people's thinking. Don't let the noise of others' opinions drown out your own inner voice. And most important, have the courage to follow your heart and intuition. They somehow already know what you truly want to become. Everything else is secondary."

Steve Jobs, Co-founder of Apple Inc (1955 – 2011)

Self-motivation, self-worth, self-respect, self-care and ultimately a self-purpose.

The former is a measure of how far we drive ourselves to achieve our goals; particularly during times of adversity.

The next three are all measures of how much we value ourselves. These measure our ability to recognise our right to be happy, to be respected, and to view ourselves and our personal achievements positively. These are collectively referred to as 'self-esteem'.

The last one is the reason for our existence: our life's purpose. It makes our lives meaningful.

The more we have of all five, the happier and more successful we are.

Self-motivation

Why do we do what we do? What drives us to get up in the mornings? To invest in relationships? To pursue a certain type of career? It is our **values**. Our values drive us every day and are the essence of self-motivation. The more we live our values on a day to day basis, the happier and more motivated we are. These values, at a sub-conscious level, drive our priorities in life. If we do not honour our values and fulfill them, we may experience a whole array of negative emotions ranging from sadness, disappointment, anger, depression, resentment and even trauma.

For example, you value being on time and are always on time when meeting a friend. This friend, however, is consistently late. You have raised the matter with them on several occasions; however, there have been no changes in their behaviour. This makes you feel that they do not appreciate how busy you are and you feel disrespected. In this case, you have a choice. You can continue the friendship as it is, or you can tell them, one last time, how you feel. If after this final plea, there are still no changes to their behaviour, then you have the option to limit the time you spend with this friend and instead, spend time with friends who do appreciate your time. I guarantee you, you will be happier with the latter option, particularly if you place a huge importance on punctuality and value your time.

Another example is one where you have strong family values and would like to spend quality time with your family after work. You are, however, battling long hours at work every week, which means that your time with them is limited. This leaves you feeling angry and you start to resent work; you start to lose your motivation in the workplace and begin to reflect this negativity at home; leading to poor quality time spent at home. This leads to a vicious cycle, perpetuating itself. It might be time to apply for a job that honours your values and gives you the work-life balance you need whilst still meeting your personal, financial and business or career goals.

Stressful situations, like the one above, are usually a product of a value conflict; and it is at this point that identifying your values can help determine the best path for you.

The important question that most people struggle with is – what are my values? For some these are obvious. For others, it may not be as straight forward. It is therefore imperative that you make a conscious effort to identify your values; and make small changes in your life to ensure you are able to live these values on a daily basis.

Identify your underlying values using the following three-step approach:

Step 1: List your values

Take a trip down 'memory lane' to times in your life when you were happy or content or just confident about life. What was it about this experience that made you feel good? And who were the people with you? What qualities did you value in these people that made you feel supported, happy or confident?

The following list will help to trigger a list of values that resonate with you. Compiling a list of at least 10 values will help you determine what activities, career goals, business objectives or relationships, you should pursue in order to ensure that you honour these values. You will find that some of these values go hand in hand with others. For example, freedom and independence are related values.

Accountability	Cooperation	Equality
Accuracy	Compassion	Enthusiasm
Achievement	Competitiveness	Excellence
Ambition	Courtesy	Fairness
Assertiveness	Creativity	Faith
Autonomy	Curiosity	Family values
Being the best	Decisiveness	Fidelity
Cautiousness	Diligence	Fitness
Challenge	Discipline	Freedom
Courage	Diversity	Goodness
Commitment	Efficiency	Grace
Community	Elegance	Gratitude
Control	Empathy	Happiness

Hard work	Openness	Selflessness
Harmony	Organisation	Security
Health	Patience	Shrewdness
Honesty	Peace	Spontaneity
Humility	Perfection	Stability
Independence	Personal Development	Status
Intelligence	Philanthropy	Strategic
Justice	Positivity	Supportive
Kindness	Pragmatism	Team work
Trustworthiness	Professionalism	Thoughtfulness
Logic	Prudence	Timeliness
Love	Reliability	Travelling
Loyalty	Religion	Vision
Obedience	Resourcefulness	Work-life Balance

This list is just an example of values that you may hold and is by no means a complete list. Therefore, I encourage you to add to this.

Step 2: Pioritise your values

Once you have identified your values, it is important to prioritise them – as there will no doubt be situations where you will need to choose between two values in order to identify the value which will make you happier or more satisfied. Rank your values starting from the most valued to the least valued, working through the above list.

This exercise is central to helping you make the right life choices and decisions that in the long-term will allow you to lead a more satisfying and rewarding life.

This may be a difficult process at first – however, using this method you can identify the top three values that make you the happiest. As long as these values are not compromised in any area of your life, you will find that you are living the life you want.

Step 3: Review your values

Certain situations or life-changing events may lead to a change in your values or priorities. For example, when you started your career or your business, hard work and commitment to your career or business may have been your top priorities; however as you start a family you may prioritise family values over work. Therefore review your values as follows:

List your existing values. Are these still important to you? Are they still in the correct order? Compare them to the full list of values you prepared in the exercise above. Are there new ones? Re-order them and again identify your top three values. These will guide you in all your life decisions and goals and prevent you from experiencing stressful or negative situations.

Whenever you feel life is challenging or things are just not working out, review and assess your most important values. This will help reinforce the confidence and clarity you need to improve your current situation.

Self-worth, self-respect and self-care (collectively known as 'self-esteem')

We hold a natural and sub-conscious assumption that our worth is dependent on how others treat us and feel about us; that is, our self-worth is based on others' opinions. This is in fact an extremely dangerous place to be. People can be fickle and today's icons will be tomorrow's falling stars, as a result of public opinion. We have heard so many of these stories in the media. If celebrities were to base their self-esteem on the public's view of them, they would be depressed and perhaps even drug addicts overcoming negative self-worth. In fact, many celebrities have fallen into this trap. To benchmark our self-worth against other people's fickle opinions is dangerous. We would be yoyos, lacking stability, focus and control over our own lives.

Instead, our self-worth, self-respect, self-care should be set by us, based on how we want to be treated and respected. We cannot control others' views and thoughts of ourselves. However, we can control our own views and thoughts of us. When we value our time, abilities and bodies, we are true to ourselves. We set our own standards of how we want to be treated and we immediately see a difference in terms of how others treat us. We are able to command a natural self-respect from others.

We are more positive about ourselves; and as a result, we are more motivated to achieve. The more we achieve, the better we feel about ourselves leading to a self-fulfilling virtuous cycle. This has significant benefits for our mental and physical health as it prevents us from being diseased with the problems that chronic stress brings.

"People often say that motivation doesn't last. Well, neither does bathing. That's why we recommend it daily."

Zig Ziglar,American Author, Salesman & Motivational Speaker (1926 -2012)

Practise self-motivation, self-worth, self-respect and self-care on a daily basis.

Value yourself every day:

- Write down your strengths.
- Acknowledge, embrace and develop your weaknesses. No one is perfect.
- Remember compliments you have received.
- Save all your positive feedback.
- Smile in the mirror every day.
- If you make a mistake, acknowledge it. Be grateful for the lesson you have learnt and move forward. Do not berate yourself too much.
- Be grateful for the wonderful things in your life.

Command self-respect:

Practise assertiveness (the ability to confidently affirm your point of view without being aggressive or submissive):

When people treat you well, treat them well too. This is akin to an unspoken 'code of conduct' that both parties mutually respect.

If people behave inappropriately with you, and you are unsure whether it is intentional, clarify this with them.

If they do it again, though, then treat them with equal discomfort or annoyance, but do not feel guilty or angry about it (and certainly do not cause mental, physical or financial harm in the process). Otherwise ignoring them only rewards the bad behaviour and the bad behaviour will only continue. As Abraham Lincoln said: 'Silence is consent.' Instead penalise the bad behaviour. This discourages the other person from repeating the negative behavior in the future. Similarly, good behaviour should be rewarded; this encourages the other person to repeat this behaviour. In this way good behavior is rewarded and repeated, whilst bad behavior is penalized and discouraged.

Promote self-care:

- Eat healthily.
- Sleep well.
- Exercise.
- Make time for things that you enjoy, whether it is socialising, watching a movie, or reading a good book.
- Meditate – I cannot overstate the power of meditation and the profound impact it can have on your mental, emotional and physical health.
- An alternative to meditation is mindfulness – the ability to focus fully on the present. The future and the past are just figments of our imaginations. What is real is what is now. Living in the past can make us depressed whilst living in the future can lead to great anxiety about the future. The power of the present helps focus our energies on things that matter. Focus on a beautiful flower that you have seen – appreciate its fragrance, its design, its colours and its vibrancy. Fully focus on it and give it the attention it deserves. Enjoy the experience and be thankful that you have had the opportunity to observe something wonderful and inspiring. Do this with any activity you enjoy.

The above activities will energise you; and give you the strength to navigate through life's challenges.

Self-purpose

Once you have identified your values using the technique above, use these to determine your purpose. Your purpose is what motivates you to get out of bed every day, what drives you to go that extra mile and what allows you to smile in the face of adversity. Living your purpose every day means living your values; it ultimately means being true to yourself.

"Living with integrity means: Not settling for less than what you know you deserve in your relationships. Asking for what you want and need from others. Speaking your truth, even though it might create conflict or tension.

Behaving in ways that are in harmony with your personal values. Making choices based on what you believe, and not what others believe."

Barbara De Angelis, American relationship consultant, Author and Television Personality

There are many of us who are not true to ourselves. We continue to pursue a career or goal that is not ours. When we do this we only let ourselves down; for not listening to our needs. We are hurting ourselves every day, that we choose to continue on a path that is not our own. This does not have to be the job or career we are following; it can be anything we do which gives us a sense of purpose and allows us to do what we are here to do. It could be looking after an elderly family member; or volunteering at a local mental health charity; or cooking delicious meals for a friend.

"What allows us, as human beings, to psychologically survive life on earth, with all of its pain, drama, and challenges, is a sense of purpose and meaning"

Barbara De Angelis, American relationship consultant, Author and Television Personality

"Strive not to be a success, but rather to be of value."

Albert Einstein, Physicist and Nobel Prize Winner (1879 – 1955)

Having a sense of purpose accelerates your motivation and self-esteem a thousand fold.

Whatever it is, find it, honour it and do it. It will change your perspective on life.

Strategy 2: Practising Creativity, a Vision Board, and an Inspiration Toolkit

"Imagination is everything. It is the preview of life's coming attractions."

Albert Einstein, Physicist and Nobel Prize Winner (1879 – 1955)

"Imagination is the beginning of creation. You imagine what you desire, you will what you imagine, and at last you create what you will".

George Bernard Shaw, Irish Playwright and Co-founder of London School of Economics (1856 – 1950)

Creativity is the single most important life skill guaranteed to bring you success. Creativity encompasses the ability to dream, to envision and to be innovative in your thinking. Think about all the countless success stories that creativity has spurred (for example, Steve Jobs and Apple, Mark Zuckerburg and Facebook, Thomas Edison and electricity).

Creativity enables you to think outside of the box. Problem-solving and innovation rely on creative skill. This enables new and unique solutions to current issues. Without this ability we are likely to hit road blocks; we may not have any new ideas for scientific and health improvements, for innovation or for education leading to a slow stagnation of the human race.

Why is creativity important to you as an individual? The ability to dream and use your imagination, helps you identify what it is that you want from life . This skill, whilst obvious, underpins our ability to set a life vision and related goals.

In fact, people are truly at one with themselves when they are expressing their true creativity. A form of self-expression, it allows you to both communicate and experience your joys, excitement and enthusiasm as well as your sorrows, frustrations and anger. It is therapeutic at worst.

I therefore urge you to practise and develop your creativity skills at every opportunity you get. Many people struggle with creativity and believe that they were not born creative and therefore will never have it in them. This is simply not true. In fact, it is a quality inherent in all of us. As Pablo Picasso famously said: *"Every child is an artist. The problem is how to remain an artist once we grow up. "*

There is no prescribed formula for creativity. What works for one person may not work for the other. It is a personal choice. I urge you to spend time developing your creative abilities, whether that is in the form of travelling, experiencing new cultures, tasting new cuisines that you have never tried before; writing a blog or a novel, painting or attending a drawing or design class. It can be anything new or creative that you have wanted to explore for a while, but have not pursued for a number of reasons.

When we experience something new we encourage right-brain thinking (the creative side). Commit yourself to a new experience: learn how to cook; experiment with food; go wine-tasting; undertake a photography course; participate in a gelato-making course; or learn how to make jewellery or perfume.

The more you practise creativity, the easier it becomes. This will only make your ability to dream big and create a vision for your life significantly easier.

Creating your life vision

"We are what we think. All that we are arises with our thoughts. With our thoughts, we create our world."

Buddha, Founded Buddhism

"Life isn't about finding yourself, life is about creating yourself".

George Bernard Shaw, Irish Playwright and Co-founder of London School of Economics (1856 – 1950)

Use the power of your imagination to design your life vision and your goals – what you would like your life to be like in the next decade or two and the goals you need to set to get there. Create a tool called a **'vision board'**. This could simply be a large canvas board with pictures from magazine cutouts, personal photos, prints or anything that inspires you and that you would like to have in a year's time, two years' time, five years' time, ten years' time or even twenty years' time. (An alternative to a vision board is an online **Pinterest** board. **Pinterest** allows users to post images of things they like on boards and categorise them as they please. This is a great tool for capturing your life vision.)

From this life vision, break it down into short-term, medium-term and long-term goals and write down the actions you need to take to achieve these goals. Commit to a time frame to complete both the actions and the goals and stick to it as much as possible. There will no doubt be unexpected events that life throws at you, which throw you off course, however, use the creative process to think outside of the box and create a solution for one that did not exist previously. This creative process allows you to actively think about exactly what you want in life and how you can make it happen.

It may be a challenge initially. Your mind might throw up reasons as to why you should not achieve these goals. Do not be discouraged by this. The key is to stay with the creative process and remember that you deserve to realise your dreams (refer to **Strategy 1** on self-worth). Where there is a will, there is a way. Therefore, during the creative process, truly believe that there are no barriers and that you will overcome any challenges you may encounter.

For example, if you want a beautiful home in a lovely location that you have always dreamed of; believe it will be yours. Take pictures of it and put it on your vision board. Associate positive feelings of happiness, excitement and exhilaration with the picture; the sort of feelings you might have if the house was already yours. Create memories of you and your partner or family in the house. The stronger the feelings and associations, the more committed and focused you become on the outcome. Your mind enters into 'thinking-outside-of-the-box' mode, creating solutions that you may never have thought about before. Using this process, you progress closer to your goal.

A powerful trick is to go to bed with any concerns or questions you have regarding how you are going to achieve your goal. The creative process will kick in overnight and you will find that the next morning you have a solution to your concern or challenge. This is a profound tool. I encourage you to make use of it whenever you hit a road block. A guided meditation tape or relaxing music combined with a visualisation of your vision board is also a powerful way to focus your mind and energies on your goals.

"You see things; and you say, 'why'? I see things and say 'Why not'?

George Bernard Shaw, Irish Playwright and Co-founder of London School of Economics (1856 – 1950)

Why should there not be a solution? Where there is a will, there is always a way.

"Twenty years from now you will be more disappointed by the things that you didn't do than by the ones you did do, so throw off the bowlines, sail away from safe harbor, catch the trade winds in your sails. Explore, Dream, Discover. "

Mark Twain, American Author and Lecturer (1835 – 1910)

Sometimes our feelings, if negative, can impact our ability to visualise our life vision or dream. We are stuck in this paralysis of negative thought and chatter that tells us it is a waste of time or it will never happen. In these instances I use something called the '**Inspiration Toolkit**' which is designed to make you feel more positive and embrace a 'winning mindset.

The Inspiration Toolkit

1. Keep hold of something that reminds you of a period in your life when you were truly happy or inspired. This could be a photo or a piece of jewellery or clothing or a book. Re-live the emotions from that memory. This will invigorate you with a new found inner confidence.

2. Keep a photo of somebody close to you, for example, your partner, your parents, a member of your family or even a close friend or confidante. You are more likely to feel confident about your goals and dreams when you know you are supported.

3. Keep hold of an item that reminds you of a time when you achieved something special or important to you. This could be a certificate, a puzzle that you have completed, a photo of a meal that you cooked or a painting that you created. This reaffirms your ability to achieve again and restores your faith in pursuing a dream with a positive outcome.

4. Include a symbol or a note of something you are aspiring towards; for example, a new language that you are learning, a business course that you are completing or a new relationship. This reminds you of the new goals in your life and that you are working towards something important to you, which is a great boost to your self-esteem.

5. Include a biography or magazine of someone who inspires you. This will inspire you as you realise that everyone has setbacks and yet they achieve wonderful things in their lives.

6. Include a ticket or email or note of an upcoming event – something that you are looking forward to. This could simply be a trip to the cinema or a new restaurant that you want to try out or even a concert performance that you want to attend; this will lift your spirits and renew the enthusiasm required to create your vision.

7. Lastly, include a thank you note, an email or a similar item that you have received from a friend or colleague that reminds you of how you helped someone in the past. This will boost your confidence in your abilities.

Be inspired every day by your inspiration toolkit; your vision board and a creative activity that you practise daily. You can achieve your dreams. Nothing is impossible. Have courage and faith in your ideas; and you will be amazed at the outcomes.

"Limitations live only in our minds. But if we use our imaginations, our possibilities become limitless."

Jamie Paolinetti, American cyclist

"The future influences the present just as much as the past."

Friedrich Nietzsche, German Philosopher (1844 – 1900)

Strategy 3: Communication and Body Language

"The single biggest problem in communication is the illusion that it has taken place."

George Bernard Shaw, Irish Playwright and Co-founder of London School of Economics (1856 – 1950)

If there is one personal development area that should top your list– it is communication. If your communication is not great, improve it. If your communication is ok, strive to become better. If your communication is great, aim to become an expert.

The long-term benefits of communication are understated. It gives life to our personal and professional relationships. It enables us to be understood as we want to be. It also gives us the power to influence and negotiate better which enables us to become better at asking for what we want.

It allows us to become better partners and parents. It improves our health and prevents chronic stress from building up as we get better at communicating our needs and managing conflict. The list is endless. There is no substitute for good communication. The professional and personal benefits of good communication far outweigh the time and money spent on it initially.

There is a whole range of tools available to improve your communication from books, blogs, newsletters, seminars, group coaching to one-to-one coaching. The amount you can afford to invest depends on both your budget and time that you have available. However, anything that you can do will be of benefit. Therefore I continue to stress that you invest the time and money in learning how to communicate better – you will be pleasantly surprised.

Communication is made up of both verbal and non-verbal elements which comprise the following:

7% is what you say; 30% is your voice; and 63% is your body language. Body language includes our postures, our facial expressions and our gestures. 'What we say' therefore is dwarfed by 'how we say it'; and 'how we say it' creates the impact we want.

Adapting your Body Language

Based on the above statistics, body language is the most important aspect of communication. Body language often reflects how you feel about what you say and whether you truly mean it. It communicates authenticity. Authenticity invokes trust in the other person. This is important.

If you do not believe what you say then your body language reveals this. The other person sub-consciously observes that something does not add up. They may not take what you say at face value; this weakens your message.

You can learn to consciously manage your facial expressions, postures and gestures. Observe yourself and become aware of how you are standing, the gestures you use and the facial expressions you make. If you are not sure – ask a trusted colleague, friend or family member to give you feedback. Once you become aware of your body language you can consciously change the way you stand or change the facial expressions and gestures you make to portray yourself in the best light when communicating.

Power postures include standing tall, chin up, shoulders back and opening up your chest to the person you are talking to. This tells the person that you are open and approachable. They are more likely to trust you and you will come across as confident and positive.

Shifting your position to appear bigger either by standing with your legs wide apart or stretching your hands into a V-shape, communicates assertiveness. Always make strong eye contact with the person you are talking to. If shaking hands, make sure that your handshake is strong and firm.

Mirroring the person you talk to is another powerful technique. Imitation is the greatest form of flattery and this has never been truer. Mirroring the other person helps to build up a strong rapport at a subconscious level. It puts the other person at ease and builds mutual trust. Mirror both, the body language as well as the pitch and tone of the voice, in a subtle manner. This establishes mutual trust and rapport.

Weak power postures include touching your neck or face. These suggest that you are feeling low or are in need of support. Not making eye contact or putting your hands in your pockets is also a sign of a lack of confidence.

Changing your body language slightly has a tremendous impact on the way you come across. Work hard to understand power postures, gestures and facial expressions. Practise these using the **conscious competence** model. Under this model, before someone learns a new skill, not only do they not know the skill, they are also unaware that they do not know the skill. This is referred to as 'unconscious incompetence'. When they start learning the new skill, they become aware of the existence of the skill that they have not yet acquired. This is known as 'conscious incompetence'. As they gradually begin to learn the skill they actively practise it and get better. This stage is referred to as 'conscious competence'. Finally, they become good at the skill and can do it in their sleep or on auto-pilot. This last stage is known as 'unconscious competence'. These principles are often used when someone first learns to drive a car. Practise makes perfect and the 'unconscious competence' stage is where you want to get to with eventual practice. Practise your gestures and postures every day to the point at which you naturally use your body language in a way that allows you to communicate effectively.

Another benefit of practicing good body language is that when you present power postures, and confident facial expressions – you psychologically change how you feel. This was demonstrated by a study conducted at the Ohio State university in 2003 which concluded that our feelings are influenced by our psychological behaviour. For example, when we sit up straight we are more likely to remember positive memories or think of something positive in general.

Therefore, by choosing power postures, not only do you communicate more confidently – you feel more confident and better about yourself. The more confident you feel about yourself, your body language adapts to reflect this. In turn, as you exhibit naturally stronger body language you come across as more confident. It becomes a virtuous cycle of positive reinforcement. Psychologists and coaches all over the world are promoting this concept more and more with clients because of its results on effective communication.

Practise the skill as often as you can and **'fake it till you make it!**' This means keep pursuing the skill as though you are already good at it. The trick lies in performing the action (focusing on the body's movements rather than focusing on whether it makes you look silly or stupid, otherwise your brain will bring up reasons as to why you cannot do it). Practise the poses regularly – it will become easier over time.

Reading others' Body Language

Body language also reveals what someone is truly thinking or how they are feeling. If we are hungry or tired – our bodies know first and a signal is subsequently sent to the brain. Therefore our body language communicates our emotions before our brain even registers how it is feeling.

Practise observing other people. Be aware of individual differences. People from different countries and cultures associate different meanings with different gestures and facial expression; bear in mind the age, culture, religion, gender, and any other relevant context when reading a person's body language. A teenager, an older woman, and a Japanese businessman are likely to use non-verbal signals differently.

"Words are a wonderful form of communication, but they will never replace kisses and punches."

Ashleigh Brilliant, British Author and Syndicated Cartoonist

Emotional awareness

Emotions and body language are connected, therefore, it is important to understand emotions. Start by understanding your own feelings as this allows you to relate to other people's emotions better. Having an awareness of how you are feeling, helps you to empathise and connect better with others. Understanding your own feelings may appear straight-forward, however, emotions such as anger, sadness, negativity can be painful to express and sometimes, it is easier to suppress them. It is essential that these feelings are expressed.

'Expressing' these emotions means recognising and acknowledging them. Do not judge them. Let them be; allow yourself to experience them in the moment. This lets you 'process' the emotion and release it. For example, if you are angry with someone, acknowledge the anger. The emotion is telling you something.

Allow yourself to be angry and express it via a medium. This could be by telling someone how you are feeling, or squeezing a stress ball really tight, or yelling loudly when no one is around. (Always do this in a safe environment as you should not hurt anyone in this process). Remember, anger can lead to depression if not expressed.

Allow your inner 'child' to be angry at the older 'adult' you for not managing the conflict or allowing yourself to be treated negatively. This is an important step. It allows you to take personal responsibility and empowers you to do something about it. Lastly, determine the best course of action so that you can move forward from this angry place.

You can do so by talking to a friend, a therapist or even expressing them through a creative activity such as drawing or dancing. This will allow you to recognise, express and acknowledge these feelings. You will find it easier to connect with and relate to someone else who may also experience these.

The Voice

Your voice comprises 30% of all communication. Therefore the tone and pitch you use to communicate has a substantial impact on how you come across. If you are like most people, you probably feel uncomfortable when hearing your own voice. However, there are tips that you can use immediately to ensure that you come across as clear, confident and interesting.

Relaxing is key. Taking a few deep breaths before an important conversation helps lower the pitch and tone of your voice. When you are nervous you may speak very fast in a high pitched voice, which loses your ability to be understood clearly and also loses authority. Low-pitched voices subconsciously have more authority.

Always pause for about 2 – 3 seconds after each sentence. This may seem like a lifetime at first, but it will help you to control your speed and avoid racing ahead of yourself. This will also appear natural to your audience as the pause gives them time to adjust to your voice and take in what you have just said.

A good way to practise pausing is to read aloud a piece of text. Mirror somebody who is a great speaker or inspires you to communicate better. This makes it easier to understand what you should be aiming for in order to come across well.

Lastly, practice makes perfect – continue to repeat these small exercises over and over again. Eventually you will master the art of eloquent communication.

Listening

Whilst the voice is 30% responsible for effective communication, listening is equally important. It makes the speaker feel heard and understood, which can help build a stronger connection between you and the speaker. This creates an environment where both parties feel safe expressing ideas, opinions and feelings. This 'safe' environment helps clarify information, avoid conflicts and misunderstandings which all save time.

It also enables the expression of negative emotions; which allows the person feeling negative to relieve the negative emotion and move to a position where both parties can begin problem solving or resolving issues.

Actively take an interest and engage in what the other person says. Maintain a non-judgmental attitude. This includes not interrupting and fully focusing on what the other person is saying. Do not think about what you are going to say next - this distracts you from what the other person is saying and they will pick up on it through your body language and facial expressions.

Effective listening, allows you to accurately interpret what the other person is saying. Be mindful of the things that are not said. Silence can also be a form of communication. This is when body language and facial cues become key.

"Most people do not listen with the intent to understand; they listen with the intent to reply."

Stephen R. Covey, American Educator, Author and Businessman (1932 2012)

The way we communicate with ourselves and with others determines the quality of our self-esteem, our relationships, our careers and business life and as a result the overall quality of our lives. Therefore, I urge you to engage in daily practice to develop and maintain your communication skills. They will transform your relationships.

"Communication works for those who work at it. "

John Powell, British Composer, Conductor and Producer

"Communication is a skill that you can learn. It's like riding a bicycle or typing. If you're willing to work at it, you can rapidly improve the quality of every part of your life."

Brian Tracy, Canadian Motivational Speaker and Author

"Take advantage of every opportunity to practise your communication skills so that when important occasions arise you will have the gift, the style, the sharpness, the clarity and the emotions to affect other people."

Jim Rohn, American Author, Entrepreneur and Motivational Speaker (1930 – 2009)

Strategy 4: Human Connections, Selective Relationships and a Supportive Network

"Man is by nature a social animal; an individual who is unsocial naturally and not accidentally is either beneath our notice or more than human. Society is something that precedes the individual. Anyone who either cannot lead the common life or is so self-sufficient as not to need to, and therefore does not partake of society, is either a beast or a god. "

Aristotle, Greek Philosopher (0322 – 0384)

Human beings are a social animal. We have an innate need to belong to a group, to inter-depend. We have a variety of needs and these can only be met through living in human society. Living in isolation means that only half of these needs are met. Therefore, through evolution, we have become animals that live in societies.

This innate need to inter-depend has evolved to the point that human-beings coexist in a highly complex society. And this constantly propels our need to belong to something bigger than ourselves. We just have to look at Facebook and Twitter to see the power of groups and the effect they can have on us. We are hooked – addicted to social networks and it is a trend that will only continue to grow. These social networks have made it incredibly easy for us to connect with others and create new relationships within seconds.

Self-awareness

Our ability to connect with others, empathise, reason, or learn a language require us to be self-aware. Self awareness cannot be developed in isolation and comes from interacting with others.

In fact how others treat us is a reflection of how we treat ourselves. If we respect ourselves, we easily command respect from others. If we value ourselves, others value us. This might be sub-conscious; however, our relationships mirror our relationship with ourselves; and this provides a vital clue to understanding our feelings, values and beliefs better. Once we are aware of our own feelings, values and beliefs we will find it easier to relate to other people's emotions, values and beliefs, positively interact with them; empathise, listen better, influence and negotiate.

Once self-aware, we can make the right choices in life to ensure that we live in line with our values and beliefs and surround ourselves with people who will have a positive impact on our lives.

Selective relationships

Who you choose to spend your time with, has a huge impact on your life. It is probably one of the most important decisions that you will make and as a result one of the hardest. Having a strong awareness of the quality of people around you is vital. It is easy to fall into friendships; it could be that your friend lives next to you. It could be that you enjoy going to concerts together. It could be that your children are friends. There is a whole host of reasons why people become friends and it is a wonderful experience. We do not choose who our family is. There are relationships that we maintain because they are blood or because we have mutual friends and do not want to make it awkward.

As a result, most people are not selective about their relationships. They go through life reacting to those around them.

However, what we do not realise is that we have a lot more power than we think to carefully choose who we want to spend time with. People who inspire and encourage us to be the best we can be; people who respect us; people who have a positive impact on our self-esteem; people who listen to us and who we can depend on in tough times; these are the people who have a positive impact on our lives.

In fact, if you want to be financially successful, then surround yourself with people who are financially successful. If you want to be healthy, then surround yourself with people who are healthy. Who you surround yourself with is a reflection of who you are. The simple rule of thumb is to surround yourself with people who have the same values as you. You will be happier and lead a richer life. (This is why the **Values** exercise outlined in **Strategy 1** is crucial in identifying your values).

Relationships that clash with your values or breed negativity are harmful in the long term. You will spend most of your time wondering how best to deal with these people. For example, people who complain all the time; people who take from the relationship, but never give in return; people who behave manipulatively and selfishly impact your self-esteem and your motivation.

Subconsciously we take on board these negative behaviours and become the negative person. Negative behaviours should be warning signs that this person may not be someone you want in your inner network of friends. If, after meeting with a friend or relative, you feel exhausted or drained, this should serve as a red flag and you should assess your relationship with this person.

If this person drains your energy you need to create space away from them. By maintaining the relationship as it is, without any feedback on their behavior or without creating space away from them, you actually reward their current behaviour.

You need to tell them the impact their behaviour has on you so that they are aware of how you feel. In the first instance if this person is someone you regard as close to you, you should make every effort to discuss their behaviour with them and tell them how you feel. Do this by feeding back how you feel every time they act in a certain way. Do not be accusatory.

For example, "I feel angry when I have been waiting for half an hour from the time we were meant to meet and I have not received a message or phone call to tell me that you are running late. I get even angrier when this happens repeatedly, particularly as I am always on time." If after this has been clearly fed back and they still continue to repeat this behaviour with no respect or value for your time, and this upsets you it is perhaps time to move on from the relationship and limit the time you spend with this person.

How do we move away from people who have been such a big part of our lives? Are we just friends with people because we have a history? Sometimes you just need a clean break. Create space. Focus all your energies on yourself and prioritise other important things in your life. Do not focus on the loss of the friendship – do not be angry, sad or feel guilty. This will only breed negativity and will mean that even though you do not see or speak to this person, they are still renting space in your head for free and making you feel negative. Instead, walk away from the friendship peacefully. Do not gossip about them, bad-mouth them to your friends or focus any of your thoughts and feelings on them. Focus on the positive in your life, on good friends, relatives and colleagues who support you.

Nurture these positive relationships. There is a growing body of evidence that suggests good relationships mean healthier and longer lives. People who have a strong support network of friends, colleagues and relatives are able to rely on them during challenging times, reducing the stress and anxiety they may be feeling. It also helps to raise self-esteem and maintain a general sense of well-being. The absence of this could reduce life expectancy or immune function or lead to depression.

Going one step further, I would recommend proactively creating a power network that not only supports you, but helps you achieve your goals and ambitions and live your values to the fullest. Diverse and quality relationships enable all your emotional needs to be met. This could range from close friends to acquaintances. This ensures that even if you lose some relationships along the way you will always have others within the network to rely on. This creates a 'community' of relationships (communities are near-extinct these days as people relocate or move to larger cities where a sense of community is absent).

There is no excuse for not building new relationships and for not nurturing existing ones: spend time getting to know people with common interests to you; perhaps at a local class or at work or through organised events such as www.meetup.com or befriending friends of friends or family. Additionally, with the flurry of social networks, the new connection you make online may end up potentially being a life changing relationship.

"The richest people in the world look for and build networks, everyone else looks for work."

Robert Kiyosaki, American Self-help Author and Motivational Speaker

Lastly, celebrate these relationships. Celebrate your relationship anniversaries with your friends, partners and family members. Write little thank you messages. Send a gift. Tell them how much they mean to you. Go on holiday. Go for a meal. Do something as a family that you all love. This nurtures and positively reinforces your relationships; they will go from strength to strength; and so will your own individual happiness and well-being.

"Celebrate what you want to see more of. "

Thomas J. Peters, American Author

"The more you praise and celebrate your life, the more there is in life to celebrate "

Oprah Winfrey, Former American Talk Show Host and Philanthropist

Strategy 5: The Art of Influence, Persuasion and Negotiation

"If you wish to win a man over to your ideas, first make him your friend. "

Abraham Lincoln, 16th President of the United States (1809 – 1865)

"One of the best ways to persuade others is with your ears - by listening to them. "

Dean Rusk, Former United States Secretary of The States (1909 – 1994)

"If people like you they'll listen to you, but if they trust you they'll do business with you. "

Zig Ziglar, American Author, Salesman & Motivational Speaker (1926 – 2012)

Influence, persuasion and negotiation are skills that we all practise every day. As friends, we influence each other. As parents, we influence our children. As employers, we influence our employees. The list goes on. In fact anyone who is in a position of trust has the ability to influence and persuade someone to take on board their personal view.

We may see these skills as manipulative or playing with someone's mind. This is simply not true. We live in a world where if we do not take charge and voice our views, someone else will voice theirs. With social media and technology empowering more and more of the public to share their opinions and views, there has never been a better time to practise and master these skills.

It is therefore vital that we become good at these skills and ensure that our own needs are not compromised at the expense of others. In fact, we should ensure through the use of these skills that we reach a win-win position for both parties. A collaborative, rather than a compromising approach. When compromise happens, each person feels like they have sacrificed something.

Influence, persuasion and negotiation do not happen overnight in one conversation. In fact, these are all iterative processes, where listening, learning and understanding someone else's views are just as crucial as voicing your own views. This takes time. I find the following approach very useful when it comes to practising my own negotiation, persuasion and influencing skills:

1. Establish credibility. This is the starting point of any attempt to influence someone and is a two-fold approach. Firstly, you must form a relationship with the other person to gain the other person's trust. You will need to have established a good relationship before you can impose or force your views on someone. Therefore, unless you have this, refrain from imposing views at the early stages of the relationship. Secondly, you must have a certain level of expertise, knowledge or sound judgment for the other person to consider your idea seriously.

2. Framing. Once you have **established credibility**, position the idea to the other person in a way that highlights the advantages of the idea to them. To do so, you will need to truly understand the values and beliefs of the other person. Spend time getting to know the other person. Ask questions to get a better insight into their values and beliefs. Carefully listen to them. (Listening is a powerful technique. In fact, people who just listen are often branded as 'really interesting' to the people who were being listened to, despite not having said a word. See **Communication and Body Language** under **Strategy 3**).

Through listening, we can understand and learn what is important to the other person. Once you have a better understanding of the person's values and needs and how the idea aligns with their values and needs; think about the best way to convey the idea by **understanding the person's preference for communication.**

3. Understand a person's preference for communication by using the **Myers-Briggs** personality type indicator assessment. This is an extremely helpful method for assessing how a person thinks, how they like ideas presented to them, their approach to understanding the world and how they make decisions. The personality type indicator, based on Carl Jung's theory of personality tests, is a must-have tool for anyone who wants to develop strong influencing, persuasion and negotiation skills.

Myers Briggs consists of 4 different preference assessments: (i) is the person an extravert or an introvert; (ii) does the person understand the world through their senses or through their intuition; (iii) does the person make decisions based on how they think (logic) or how they feel; and (iv) does the person commit to decisions immediately or do they change their decisions as more information is received.

(i) Under the first assessment, **determine whether the person interacts with the world through their actions and behavior or if they prefer to live in a private world, by reflecting on their inner thoughts.** Does the person think out loud or does the person think before they speak and have generally prepared what they are going to say beforehand? If the person likes to interact with the external world through their actions and behavior and think out loud, then they are considered to have a preference for extraversion. You will find it easier to engage in dialogue with extraverts and understand what they think and what their questions are. At the end of the conversation with the extravert, you can expect to have a reasonable response from them in terms of their views and thoughts about the idea you have just presented to them.

If the person prefers to reflect internally on what you have said and perhaps needs to take away their thoughts before coming back to you, they most likely have a preference for introversion. With introverts, it is best to give them time to think about your idea and not push them for a decision. Give them the space and time they need to reflect and set a time frame to speak to them again to understand their final thoughts on your idea. They will give you a concise and clear response having had time to think about it and are unlikely to be persuaded away from their final answer.

(ii) Determine whether the person understands the world through their senses or through their intuition based on past experiences.

A person who has a preference for using their senses to understand the world, are practical and prefer to live in the moment. They prefer details to concepts.

A person who has a preference for using their intuition, holds a big picture view of the world. They are not interested in the details. They make sense of the world by identifying patterns.

When influencing someone who uses their senses, give them a practical experience; give them details and a day-to-day plan with steps on how you plan to implement the idea. Do not give them concepts or strategies as they will not respond to these well.

For those who prefer to use their intuition, use analogies, metaphors, strategies or concepts to explain your idea. Allow them to use their imagination. Do not give details unless asked.

For example, you would like your friend to come with you to a comedy show to see a comedian they have never seen before. For someone who uses their senses, they are more likely to be persuaded to come if you show them a video on YouTube of the comedian. For someone who uses their intuition you are more likely to persuade them by comparing them positively to their favourite comedian.

You will always have those people who are borderline; they don't have a strong preference for either. For these people, either approach is appropriate.

Understanding people's preferences takes time and practice. The more you do it, the better you will become.

(iii) Connect with the person emotionally or logically depending on their preference.

Observe the person's language; does the person consistently refer to their feelings? Or do they discuss how something makes logical sense?

For the former, it is important to connect your idea to the person emotionally. For example, a person might say: "I decided to buy this house based on my gut feeling – I just knew it was the one for us". They will talk abstractly about their decision and use their intuition as a reference for why they made a certain decision.

Someone who uses logic might say: "It made sense to buy this house. It was close to all the schools and public transport links. It was perfect for what we wanted".

Once you know whether the person has a preference for emotion or logic, you can use relevant language to appeal to either their emotional brain or their logical one.

The more you start observing language and thought process around decision-making the more you will readily start matching your language to the other person. Eventually you will be able to do it with your eyes closed.

(iv) Understand how the person makes decisions. Do they conclude on a decision once a specific set of information has been provided or do they make slower decisions and are prone to change as more information is received?

People who make decisions shortly after a specific set of information has been provided, use their judgment. They make decisions quickly and tend to commit to a course of action once a decision has been made. They are organised and structured, creating plans to achieve their goals and desired results in a predictable way. Approach these people with the idea and request that they get back to you as soon as possible with a decision. They most likely will come back promptly. Be consistent with them and stick to a timetable that you may have agreed.

People who adapt as more information is received like to keep their options open so that they can accommodate any issues or challenges that present themselves along the way. They like freedom and need personal space to think through the decision; they do not like to be pressured into making a decision.

They are not likely to give you a response straight away; for these people set a time frame within which they must get back to you (having had time to think through their options).

As with all preferences, there will be those who are borderline; with them you may have to use the other Myers-Briggs Indicators to effectively influence or persuade them to your view point.

Myers Briggs is an excellent tool when it comes to influencing, persuading and negotiating and I urge you to practise it on family members, friends, colleagues – with experience you will become good at identifying people's preferences for communicating with the world, understanding it and making decisions.

This four step approach is infallible: Build good relationships, ask the right questions and consistently apply the above strategy. In time, you will master the art of influence, persuasion and negotiation.

"So much of life is a negotiation, so even if you're not in business, you have opportunities to practise all around you."

Kevin O'Leary, Canadian Businessman and Television Personality

Strategy 6: The Power of Resilience and Not Sweating the Small Stuff!

I've missed more than 9000 shots in my career. I've lost almost 300 games. 26 times I've been trusted to take the game winning shot and missed. I've failed over and over and over again in my life. And that is why I succeed.

Michael Jordan, Former American Professional Basketball Player

What is resilience? It is the ability to bounce back from tough times; a quality that allows you to persevere in the face of adversity. Resilience has never been a key focus for psychologists – however recently it has attracted significant attention. Previously it has only ever been acknowledged by doctors who observed that patients who remained calm about serious illnesses recovered the quickest.

With the global financial crisis in 2007, resilience attracted more interest. It was a time of turmoil for many who lost their jobs, their livelihoods both psychologically and financially. It tested the personal resilience of many and it highlighted how some people deal significantly better with negative changes than others.

We live in a world where we face ever increasing challenges, conflicts and competition. Our survival and well-being is dependent on this skill. Some people naturally develop this as they grow up during difficult periods in their childhood or young adulthood; some hit crisis point and learn to develop it over time. The good news is that anyone can develop or 'learn' resilience with the right tools.

Below are examples of famous people who faced huge adversity in their lives and yet went on to become some of the most successful:

Career setbacks

Michael Jordan: One of the greatest basketball players of all time. He was rejected from his high school basketball team for being undersized He rose above it and persevered to become arguably one of the best in the world in his field.

Walt Disney: He perhaps tells the greatest success stories of resilience. Walt Disney faced countless rejections with one employer citing that he lacked imagination and did not have any good ideas. Despite this he went on to set up businesses which again failed and went bankrupt. He then went on to create the Disney theme parks and movies. He received four honorary Academy Awards and won twenty-two Academy Awards out of a total fifty-nine nominations; more than any other individual in history.

J. K. Rowling: Rowling lived in a council flat. She was a divorced, depressed single mother of one struggling to make ends meet. Despite this she continued to write the Harry Potter series, which has now made her one of the richest women on the planet. She achieved this over 5 years through sheer hard work, determination and perseverance.

Albert Einstein: He could not speak until he was three years old and could not read until seven years old. His parents and teachers were concerned that he was mentally disabled. Despite this slow start, he won a Nobel Prize in Modern Physics and became an international symbol of genius.

Health setbacks

Michael J. Fox: A huge TV and movie star best known for his performances in the "Back to the Future" movie series, was diagnosed with Parkinson's disease at 30 years old (most cases develop at 50 years). Parkinson's disease is a degenerative neurological disorder of the central nervous system and impacts a person's ability to walk and leads to physical handicap.

His diagnosis was only made public 7 years later. During this time he re-framed his attitude to Parkinson's, became an advocate for other sufferers and set up a health foundation in search of a cure for the condition; committed to raising research funding and awareness of the condition.

Oscar winning actress **Halle Berry** was diagnosed with diabetes in 1989, at 22 years old. She is now 45 and manages it with regular exercise and a healthy diet. Despite this she went on to win an Oscar for her performance in Monster's Ball and is the mother of two.

Nick Cannon, the host of "America's Got Talent" and Mariah Carey's husband, was diagnosed with Lupus Nephritis at age 31. Lupus nephritis is an autoimmune condition that causes chronic inflammation of the kidneys.

However, this has only inspired him to live a more meaningful life - he remains optimistic about advances in health and has faith that he can live to old age by managing his condition properly. He knows what his top priorities are: his children and his ambitions to continue pursuing a successful career.

His advice on the **www.lupus.org** website to anyone suffering from a chronic disease is: *"Get as much education on the disease as possible. That helps build your self-esteem and your confidence. The more you know and the better you take care of yourself the easier it is to deal with."*

So what is it about those who bounce back and return even stronger versus those who struggle to recover from life's challenges?

Research has shown that those who manage adversity well exhibit the following behaviour:

- Proactively problem solve and look for solutions to improve their position.

- Identify opportunities in the face of challenges.

- Recognise the need to adapt – to do things differently (champion change).

- Are resourceful. They identify where to look for support and get the help they need.

- Find a sense of purpose and meaning of life - see **Strategy 1.**

- Practise optimism.

- Manage stress and anxiety - see **Strategy 9.**

- Take responsibility for their life.

- Demonstrate good self-esteem – see **Strategy 1.**

- See failure as a form of helpful feedback.

Regardless of where you fall in the above spectrum of qualities, you can increase your resilience:

- Identify your goal – imagine that you have achieved it. Think about how you will feel when you have achieved it.

- Use your inspiration toolkit (as per **Strategy 2**). Employ a 'winning' mindset. You are on a path to success and will bounce back from wherever you are.

- Become resourceful and put your 'problem-solving hat' on. What actions do you need to take to achieve your goal? Who can help you? How can you get the assistance that you need? Explore, research and set a plan of action and timetable and stick to it.

- In the meantime, manage your stress and anxiety. (Refer to **Strategy 9**). Remember, you can only control things that are in your 'circle of influence'; that is, do not beat yourself up about the things that are out of your control. Only focus on the things that you can control and change. By doing so, you allow your mind to be freed up substantially from the clutter of unnecessary and useless worry ready to focus on the important things.

"Don't worry about the future; or worry, but know that worrying is as effective as trying to solve an algebra equation by chewing bubblegum."

Baz Luhrman, Australian Film Director, Screenwriter and Producer

- Spend time grieving losses, healing from setbacks and actively nurturing hope (Refer to **Strategy 8**). Write down how you feel. Express your grief in writing. This is an extremely powerful technique to relieve yourself of the emotion. Talk to a close confidante, whether it is a friend, a coach, a therapist or mentor. The release of the emotion brings about a sense of relief and lightens the burden.

- Surround yourself with good people and people who can help you. (Refer to **Strategy 4**) Remove any negativity and negative people. In this time of adversity, it is even more important to surround yourself with people who inspire you, motivate you and help you be the best you can be.

- Trust – have faith and believe that it will happen. The power of belief is underestimated. It is necessary for recovery. Take control and expect good things to happen. It will only be a matter of time until they will.

- Remember to be true to yourself. Live your values and your purpose. (Refer to **Strategy 1**).

"You have to trust in something - your gut, destiny, life, karma, whatever. This approach has never let me down, and it has made all the difference in my life."

Steve Jobs, Co-founder of Apple Inc (1955-2011)

Psychologists, life coaches and therapists across the world recognise the importance of resilience for survival and recovery in a world where everyone is faced with their fair share of both adversity (we all undergo some sort of stress, trauma, loss, grief or illness in our lives) and opportunities. Our success largely depends on whether we can eventually reach the light at the end of the tunnel; by using our resilience and faith to direct ourselves out of the dark tunnel. Whilst we tend to rely on this quality more during our darkest times; we must have access to it readily and invest the time in learning resilience and bouncing back stronger every time we fall.

"Good judgment comes from experience. Experience comes from bad judgment."

Jim Horning, American Computer Scientist (1942 – 2013)

"The greatest glory in living lies not in never falling, but in rising every time we fall."

Nelson Mandela, Anti-apartheid Revolutionary and Former President of South Africa (1918 -2013)

Strategy 7: Grieving and Nurturing Hope

"There is a saying in Tibetan, 'Tragedy should be utilised as a source of strength.' No matter what sort of difficulties, how painful experience is, if we lose our hope, that's our real disaster."

Dalai-Lama, Formerly known as 'Tenzin-Gyatso', 14th Dalai Lama and Spiritual and Temporal Leader of Tibet.

"Once a person is determined to help themselves, there is nothing that can stop them."

Nelson Mandela, Anti-apartheid Revolutionary and Former President of South Africa (1918 – 2013)

Sometimes life throws unexpected situations or events our way which create a huge sense of loss or sadness in our lives. These situations can shatter the world as we know it; suddenly from a place of great stability we find ourselves in an overwhelming position, experiencing overpowering emotions that we have never experienced before. This is unfamiliar territory and throws us off course. One of the most difficult situations to deal with is when we experience a deep loss; this could be when someone close to us passes away; when we lose a significant aspect of our health; we lose our jobs; experience a loss of a relationship either through a break-up, divorce, death; finding out that our partner has been disloyal; loss of a friendship; loss of financial stability; or moving away from home for the first time or relocating. The list is endless.

Grief is the natural reaction to loss. It is a deep emotion and when we experience it for the first time; it is heart-breaking. No one ever tells us how to deal with it; it is foreign, alien and difficult to understand how to shake off the sadness that refuses to shift.

We must allow ourselves to grieve; we must feel the pain to heal and to overcome the sorrow we face. Suppressing it will not make it go away; it will only resurface later. We should take as long as we need to process the grief, pain and sadness. Expressing grief leads to healing and relief from the pain of loss. The good news is that it will heal over time; and with hope. The power of time and hope help us to overcome grief; leaving us feeling stronger, more resilient and better able to deal with it if we ever experience it again.

In 1969, psychiatrist **Elisabeth Kübler-Ross** introduced her theory of the **'Five stages of grief'** in her book **'On Death and Dying'**. These are by no means set in stone and not everyone experiences them sequentially:

1. Denial. This is the first stage of the grieving process. This new reality that we face does not feel real. We experience disbelief, hoping to wake up from a bad dream; and we create another alternative explanation for what has happened to us. It is a defense mechanism that protects us from the pain of the shock as we slowly start to process what has happened.

2. Anger – During the second stage of the grieving process, we gradually realise that the loss is real; it slowly sinks in that we have lost something precious to us. We start to experience anger – "why did this have to happen to me? It's not fair! Who is to blame for this?" We do not know what to make of it or how to react. We are overwhelmed and this is expressed in the form of anger.

3. Bargaining – At this stage we attempt to negotiate with someone who may be able to change the situation or prevent it from occurring. This stage may occur prior to the loss or after the loss has happened. We focus intensely on what we could have done to avoid this situation and how wonderful life could have been if this situation had not occurred. This stage can lead to various emotions ranging from anger, guilt and fear. Resistance to what has happened only delays the healing process.

4. Depression – This is the stage when we begin to accept the loss, however it leads to feelings of sadness and despair as to what has happened. We may not want to spend time with anyone and possibly want to disconnect from loved ones to further limit any pain or suffering. Expressing the emotions and truly allowing ourselves to grieve and release these feelings helps to make room for the final stage of acceptance.

5. Acceptance This stage is probably the hardest to get to. However, once we are at this point, there is a sense of hope again as we have accepted what has happened. This is by no means a happy phase – we have been through a profound series of emotions. We have slowly started to heal. We are at peace with what has happened and we have found our closure.

During the grieving process it is really important to connect with others, whether this is with family members, friends, a counsellor, a support group, or a faith organisation. It is important to express your feelings and talk it through; and more importantly feel supported. (Refer to **Strategy 4).**

This includes surrounding yourself with positive people who support you; looking after your physical health; eating and sleeping well. Self-care is vital and I urge you not to compromise on this. Expressing your emotions in creative ways, for example through art therapy is a powerful way to grieve. There may be times when you may feel your grief more intensely – for example, birthdays, anniversaries, seeing somebody or visiting places that remind you of the loss.

During these times, spend it with people who care about you or plan to do something that will enable you to feel more positive about what has happened. For example – if it is a death of a loved one, then it could be spending time with those close to you and celebrating the person's life or doing something they would have loved.

Nurturing Hope

Hope is a powerful emotion – it motivates us to achieve, to progress, to build relationships, to create a better life for our children or to live a higher purpose. In a world where we face challenges day in and day out; hope is what keeps us going, what inspires life and allows us to accept and move forward so that we can fulfill our dreams in the face of adversity.

Hope is, in fact, a more powerful emotion than happiness as it enables us to experience happiness using our imagination. We can dream and create a vision of happiness that we would like to see in our future. We have complete power to choose exactly how we would like to experience happiness in the future.

It is central to the theme of creation; this ability to wish for something and create goals to fulfill this wish.

Without it, we would live a mediocre life; with no aspirations or ambitions. We would not make plans to realise our dreams and move past setbacks. Hope protects us from negative emotions such as depression, anger and sadness which can take a toll on both your mental and physical health.

It is critical that we introduce the daily practice of hope in our lives. Increase hope in your life by:

Setting aside 5 – 10 minutes a day where you can fully focus on yourself. Use this time to pray, meditate, visualise or focus on your vision board (refer to **Strategy 2**). During this time truly believe that you can achieve the goals that you have set and that amazing things are coming your way. I find that the morning is the best time to do this as it sets the tone for the day and you start your day feeling positive and in a 'winning mindset'. You find that you are energised to tackle the day effectively and are resistant to negativity. It allows you to preserve feelings of happiness. **Research suggests that success is 80% how you feel and 20% skill**. Therefore, it is important to be feeling good (positive, hopeful, happy, excited) to ensure that you perform your daily tasks well and prevent any negative emotions from jeopardising the end result.

Reducing the amount of news that you expose yourself to. Whilst it is important to be up-to-date with current affairs and lifestyle events – limit how much of it you absorb. News can be very negative and it subconsciously impacts how you feel.

Practising gratitude every day. (Refer to **Strategy 11**). Make a gratitude list of all the wonderful things in your life. Appreciate these things every day. Write a thank you note to someone expressing your gratitude for something that they may have helped you with or if they supported you through a difficult time. Tell someone how much you love them and how much they mean to you. You will be amazed at how powerful this can be. The more we remind ourselves of the good things in our lives; the easier it is to imagine and hope for more of these good things. It also shifts the mood from negative emotion to positive emotion.

Supporting a charity or your local community. Volunteer at a local charity or community event. Go and visit someone elderly in a care home. Donate clothes or items that you no longer need to your local charity shop. Be part of a campaign supporting a cause that you believe in. Do something that will make a difference to their lives. By giving someone else hope, you reinforce your belief in your own hopes and dreams. You are creating a positive experience for someone else and yourself; this energy is infectious. It motivates you to create a better world for yourself and others.

Hope is probably one of the most endearing and empowering of emotions. It gives us the capacity to live again when we have lost something precious. It gives us the capacity to heal and fully recover from our loss. It shifts our perspective of life and gives us the courage we need to get through our darkest hours so that we may experience joy and happiness again.

A lesson for all of us is that for every loss, there is victory, for every sadness, there is joy, and when you think you've lost everything, there is hope.

Geraldine Solon, American Author

"All human wisdom is summed up in two words; wait and hope."

Alexandre Dumas, French Writer (1802-1870);

The great essentials for happiness in this life are something to do, something to love and something to hope for.

Joseph Addison, English Essayist, Poet, Playwright and Politician (1672-1719)

Strategy 8: Creating More Time and Capacity In Your Life to Increase Productivity

Don't say you don't have enough time. You have exactly the same number of hours per day that were given to Helen Keller, Pasteur, Michelangelo, Mother Teresa, Leonardo da Vinci, Thomas Jefferson, and Albert Einstein.

H. Jackson Brown, American Author

Time is a finite resource – there will never be enough time! It is how you manage your time that is more important. The benefits of managing time effectively prevent the build of up stress and anxiety and give you the satisfaction of having full control of your life.

Your 'to-do' list is never going to go away. Eliminating your 'to-do' list should never be the goal - a busy 'to do' list means that you have goals to achieve (which is a good thing). Instead, *prioritising* goals and objectives is more helpful. Actively prioritise goals and objectives into tasks that should be completed today and those that can be completed on another day. Use deadlines and commitments as a guide to help you order these in terms of priority.

The following guidelines will help you better organise your day and create more capacity for the things that you love and enjoy.

1. Are you a planner or are you a 'spontaneous, go-with-the-flow type'?

Planners tend to organise their time into 'work' time and 'play' time (the latter refers to spending time with family or friends and doing activities that you love). If you are a planner and more tasks are added to your list, reprioritise your day – are there things that you can push back to tomorrow? Do not let the schedule be set in stone as it will only create stress and anxiety if you cannot fit it all in. If you need more time to complete a task, acknowledge it; determine the next best thing you can do about it. Do not beat yourself up over it as it will only create negativity.

If you are about to miss a deadline – do not panic. Accept it and complete as much as you can. You might be pleasantly surprised that the amount of work you have completed is more than enough. If someone suggests an alternative then listen to it without interrupting or dismissing it. It might actually be a more helpful suggestion. If your current plan is not working, then do not be afraid to re-evaluate your plan and try something new. Sometimes the best opportunities come up at the last minute.

If you are a **'spontaneous, go-with-the-flow type'**, to prevent you from feeling overwhelmed and allow you to regain control, make a plan at the start of each day – prioritise your tasks for today and your tasks for the next few days. Remember, if you can push back anything to tomorrow or another day, then reschedule it for a more helpful time. This gives you sufficient time to get the things that you need to get done today whilst creating capacity for anything else that you may need to accommodate later.

As a **'spontaneous, go-with-the-flow type'** you might be keen to change your plan if something better comes along - however it might be better to stick with the original plan; it will ensure that you complete your task on time.

Have there been times when not thinking ahead meant that you ended up wasting more time later? It might pay to do some research and due diligence about the task beforehand and plan accordingly to ensure you do not get penalised later.

2. Remember the day goes faster than you think it will.

Only plan on working a maximum of four to five hours a day; and always build in a buffer for the unexpected. Remember, spending more time on a task does not guarantee that it will be of better quality. Work smarter and you can produce higher quality in a shorter space of time.

Do not 'multi-task'. Academic studies have found that 'multi-tasking' exhausts our brain energy more quickly than if we were just focusing on one or two tasks.

Set yourself deadlines to complete tasks. We are more likely to focus if we have limited time in which to complete a task. Do not aim to work into the night; this gives the illusion that you have lots of time to complete your task, and paradoxically you will procrastinate. Instead, aim to finish by 5pm or shift it to the next day.

Do not target perfection. Instead, aim for 'good-enough'. You will be surprised at how much more you will complete whilst still ensuring the quality of the work.

Lastly, remember the **Pareto principle**: you achieve 80% of the results through 20% of the effort. For example, 80% of a clothing company's revenue comes from 20% of its client base; therefore you should focus on building and maintaining brand loyalty for this 20% of the client base.

3. Build in sufficient breaks and space from tasks.

Surprisingly, you are more productive when you have taken a break and your mind is refreshed. Have fun things to do and look forward to; to keep you motivated and working more effectively. Take that break if you need it and use it to relax and switch off. Do not stress about taking a break.

4. Build up a sense of achievement 'early on' in the day.

By getting some easy and quick tasks completed at the start of the day, we build up a sense of achievement which encourages us to get more things completed and motivates us to complete the rest of our goals for the day.

5. Identify what times of the day you 'think' best and what times of the day you 'do' best.

'Thinking' and 'Doing' are two separate processes. Do not try and do both things at once. You will find that you are far more efficient once you have thought about your approach to your work. You then just have to execute it.

Using the same process, identify the best time for you to schedule meetings (for example, when you 'think' best) and the best time to complete tasks (when you are focused and more likely to be productive).

6. Delegate and learn to make use of other people.

If there are things that someone else can do better or even do eighty percent as well as you then delegate it. Your time is better spent on things where you can add value and that only you can do. Delegating to someone else will create time and space for you to focus on these things.

7. Only focus on today and tomorrow.

If you had a bad day yesterday, do not focus on it. Learn your lesson on how it could have been better and move forward. Otherwise the negativity will jeopardise your ability to focus on the task at hand.

8. Add pleasure and meaning to tasks in order to increase your motivation to complete things on time.

Change your perception of the activities that we do not enjoy. For example, if you dislike going to the supermarket to do the weekly shop, take a friend with you. Alternatively, add an item to your shopping list that you really enjoy (for example chocolate) and look forward to buying it.

Reward yourself when you have completed a task or met a deadline or finished something that you found challenging. Have little treats to look forward to once you have completed the work, whether it is a trip to the cinema, a glass of wine or a new purchase at the mall.

9. Have a back-up plan for 'time killers'.

There will be times when a friend is running late or you are waiting in a queue or the train is stuck in the tracks. These moments can be incredibly frustrating, particularly when you have a busy schedule and an ever-increasing 'to do' list. During these times have tasks that you can complete whilst you are waiting. This could be catching up on emails, finishing that book on your Kindle or returning a call. Today's world of mobile technology makes this virtually effortless.

10. Learn to say 'no'

Saying 'no' is not an easy task – we fear that we may offend someone, or appear unhelpful or it just does not sit well with our moral code when someone needs help. We may feel guilty or fear that it will lead to conflict or that the person will not return the favour if ever you needed it.

Saying 'no' is powerful and empowers you to gain control and eliminate tasks that will only distract you from the tasks that are important to you. Learn to say 'no' and not feel guilty or anxious about it.

It will boost your confidence and to some extent people will respect you for it. They know where they stand with you and if you genuinely cannot take on a task, they will appreciate your honesty.

A helpful approach to saying 'no' is to **acknowledge** the person's request, **empathise** with them and **be firm and say no with a reason** to explain why you cannot do the task at hand. Lastly, end by suggesting an alternative approach that they can take which might help them achieve the outcome that they want.

This approach shows that you care about their interests and want to help; and explains why you cannot fulfil this particular request on this specific occasion. Ending with a helpful suggestion moves the conversation from a negative position to a positive one.

"We need to find the courage to say NO to the things and people that are not serving us if we want to rediscover ourselves and live our lives with authenticity."

Barbara De Angelis, American relationship consultant, Author and Television Personality

11. Dealing with time poor people who are holding you back

Sometimes it is people who hold us back from meeting our goals. They are either really busy, really difficult to get hold of, or you are just not on top of their priority list. How do you deal with this?

You need to make it attractive for them to spend time with you. Give them a good reason to meet with you. Appeal to their ego; compliment them and make them feel good when they are in your company. Continue to persist.

If you meet with them; plan to have your meeting over a meal and keep it short. You are helping them kill two birds with one stone; they need to eat and they also need to see you. Secondly, food makes the whole experience more enjoyable and you are more likely to appeal to them sub-consciously.

12. Dealing with too many meetings

Be clear about the purpose of the meeting. Always ask for a very, very brief agenda for the meeting to determine whether a meeting is actually required. If not, then keep the meeting as short as possible by: getting the right people in the room to start with; and keeping it focused by having someone chair the meeting.

The above techniques and approaches are designed to make us aware and mindful about how we spend our time so that we can use it more effectively and achieve more. Time is a finite currency, use it wisely. Do not let other people spend it; value it and you will be amazed at how much you can do with it.

"Don't spend a dollar's worth of time on a ten cent decision."

Peter Turla, Time Management Expert

"I am not a product of my circumstances. I am a product of my decisions."

Stephen R Covey, American Educator, Author and Businessman (1932 2012)

Strategy 9: Creating Well-being and Saying Goodbye to Stress and Anxiety

The concept of total wellness recognises that our every thought, word, and behaviour affects our greater health and well-being. And we, in turn, are affected not only emotionally but also physically and spiritually."

Greg Anderson, Former Professional Australian Player

Well-being, a generic term, captures the following concepts:

- Living a good quality of life.
- Having a positive life experience and being optimistic.
- Maintaining optimum health.
- Being self-fulfilled and satisfied.

It is subjective and varies from individual to individual. However, we have basic human needs, which, if met can lead to a sense of well-being and overall happiness and create an environment conducive to success. These are:

- **Eating well**: maintaining a balanced, nutritious diet.

- **Sleeping Well**: sleeping a minimum of 7 hours to 8 hours.

- **Fitness:** exercising regularly.

- **Freedom from stress and anxiety**: for some, this means active management of stress and anxiety on a daily basis with the use of appropriate relaxation techniques. For others, they naturally manage stress and anxiety as part of their general attitude to life.

- **Having healthy social interactions and good relationships** (refer to **Strategy 4**)

- **A sense of purpose and self-esteem (refer to Strategy 1)**

- **A sense of optimism and hope** (refer to **Strategy 7**)

- **Resilience** (refer to **Strategy 6**)

How do we ensure that we are fulfilling these needs?

Eating well

Whilst we are lucky that we live in a time where we have access to a wide range of food and drink, the variety of food choices makes it difficult to determine what is actually nutritious and promotes overall good health.

There are an enormous number of nutritiously poor foods (for example, foods that are high in saturated fat or contain added salt or sugar) out there that are readily available and affordable.

This promotes excess consumption of these foods, arguably triggering chronic illnesses ranging from obesity, to diabetes, to other auto-immune conditions.

As a result, it is important to take control of what we eat and expose our precious bodies to. Invest time in educating yourself about which foods you should be eating.

The internet has a wealth of information, on good food and healthy eating recipes. Many of the government websites outline guidelines on what foods are considered healthy and how much of it you should have.

For example, the UK National Health Services (**NHS**) website (**http://www.nhs.uk/livewell/healthy-eating/Pages/Healthyeating.aspx**) has a whole host of useful information; as well as the following US Government website (**http://www.usa.gov/Citizen/Topics/Health/Food.shtml**).

Plan your meals and eat at regular times. This will prevent you from reaching out for the wrong types of foods when hungry. Do not skip breakfast. Have a bowl of oatmeal or porridge for breakfast with skimmed milk, low fat milk or yoghurt together with some raw fruit.

Regular meals and calorie consumption, reduce the 'stress' on our pancreas, the organ responsible for producing insulin and maintaining our blood sugar levels.

Choose deserts based on fruit, low fat milk or yoghurt. If you enjoy foods such as chocolate or alcohol or anything else that is not considered the most nutritious, consume small portions of it as part of an overall balanced diet.

Aim to eat with others rather than by yourself or in front of the TV. Eating by yourself or in front of the TV promotes convenience foods such as take-out. Eating with others means that you are more likely to eat a variety of foods which gives you access to more nutrients.

Ensure that you drink at least two to three litres of water a day. Water comprises sixty percent of our body weight. It is vital to the healthy functioning of the body: removing toxins from our body, transporting nutrients and maintaining a moist environment for our our eyes, nose, throat, ear and mouth. Insufficient water leads to dehydration and as a result, tiredness. This lack of energy is not conducive to a productive working environment and can lead to stress and anxiety. Replenish your body with water regularly; you will find that it makes a huge difference to your energy levels and mood.

Making positive food choices and taking control of your health will leave you feeling more energised and positive; which in turn will allow you to achieve more. Remember to treat yourself as a little reward for making small improvements to your diet and food choices.

Sleeping well

Do not underestimate the power of sleep. When other responsibilities or activities in our life take over, we tend to compromise on sleep. The reality is that even a small loss of sleep takes a toll on your mood, energy, and ability to handle stress. It reduces your immunity and makes you susceptible to chronic conditions such as heart disease and diabetes. Sleep deprivation also leads to over-eating and weight gain to compensate for the loss of energy caused by the lack of sleep.

Good quality sleep leads to mental sharpness, productivity, emotional balance, creativity, physical vitality, and weight loss. With so many benefits, it would be crazy not to sleep more, particularly as it requires negligible effort.

How many hours of sleep do you need? The best way to determine how many hours of sleep you need is by observing how you are feeling throughout the day. If you are sleeping enough, you will feel energetic and attentive all day from the time you wake up in the morning to the time you go to sleep. You need more sleep if you are experiencing the following:

- You need naps during the day or need to sleep in on weekends.

- Have a tendency to fall asleep while watching TV.

- Struggle to get out of bed in the morning.

- Feel lethargic in the afternoon.

- Feel drowsy at work.

In order to fit in more sleep, do the following:

- **Prioritise sleep.** This should be on the top of your 'to-do' list. Commit to getting into bed by a certain time every night.

- **Commit to sleeping at least eight hours every night.** It is important to be consistent. Do not fall behind on this. If you lose ten hours of sleep over a week; increase the amount you sleep by an hour or two hours every night over the next week. If you have had chronic sleep loss, then take some time out to catch up on sleep. Go to bed at the same time every night and allow yourself to wake up naturally. Do not use an alarm clock or snooze button. Eventually you will feel energised again and will have caught up on your sleep.

- **Minimise artificial lights when sleeping.** The body inhibits production of melatonin (a hormone that helps you fall asleep at night) during the day so that you can be alert and attentive. Additional light at night, disturbs the balance of melatonin production at night; resulting in insufficient melatonin and leading to a lack of sleep. The cycle, therefore, must be sufficiently regulated with maximum melatonin at night (minimal light) and minimum melatonin during the day (maximum light).

A refreshing sleep each night puts you in good stead to start the next day, feeling positive and happy.

Fitness & Exercise

The benefits of fitness and exercise are two-fold. Not only do they keep you physically fit and prevent the onset of conditions such as heart disease, diabetes and obesity; they also help to maintain a state of happiness with the release of endorphins and prevent stress.

Fitness and exercise have become more and more critical with the increasing adoption of the sedentary lifestyle.

Any type of moderate activity is beneficial. These include running, walking, dancing, swimming, pilates, yoga, Zumba or any other activity which works out your body and heart. Experts recommend 30 minutes of activity, 5 times a week.

Freedom from stress and anxiety

Stress normally occurs as a result of an event that leads to a loss of control in our lives or a feeling of helplessness, hopelessness or loss that we struggle to move forward from. Anxiety is a reaction to 'what may be'. It is a reaction to a negative outcome that we imagine in the future. We might do this subconsciously and are unaware of this.

Both can seriously paralyse our ability to function normally if not dealt with in a timely manner. The good news is that we can learn to prevent or manage anxiety and stress so that they do not constrain us from living life to the fullest.

The following techniques will help you manage both of them effectively:

Identify your circle of influence. Determine what you can change and control - what is in your circle of influence. Focus on these things and see how you can improve your current circumstance. Let go of things outside of this circle of influence; accept that you can do nothing about them.

Build strong boundaries. Boundaries effectively set limits based on your values (refer to the **Values exercise** in **Strategy 1**). Boundaries communicate to others the things that you will tolerate and the things that conflict with your values and you will not do. These are absolutely essential to your healthy physical and mental functioning. Boundaries allow you to be true to yourself, which is important for your own peace of mind and self-esteem.

Do not let emotions such as anger, guilt, or fear compel you to compromise on your boundaries. Learn to say 'no' without feeling guilty or fearful. Be assertive: be direct and if it is impossible for you to meet someone else's deadline then let them know. If you are unhappy about someone or something – communicate this to the relevant person or someone who can help. Clarify things that are unclear. Manage your commitments; do not commit to anything that you cannot deliver on.

Plan ahead and be open to change. Do not be afraid to create space or eliminate things from your life that are causing stress; for example, changing jobs, withdrawing from a negative relationship or simply clarifying something that has been bothering you for some time.

Learn from your mistakes and do not berate yourself too much about them. No one is perfect. In fact mistakes are the building blocks for success – an expert is someone who has made every single mistake in the field.

Relaxation techniques. Find a relaxation technique that works for you. For example: listening to music; watching a movie; reading a book; walking; swimming; exercising; meditation; yoga; and massages. The list is endless. Learn to practise these daily. Remember, it takes 21 days to create a habit. Relaxation techniques should be incorporated into a habit through daily practice over at least 21 days.

Manage conflict. Do not avoid it. If you need to raise an issue with someone – do it straightaway. Do not leave it as it will only get worse. When discussing an issue with someone identify your needs and the other person's needs. Determine whether you can reach a win-win situation. Do not accommodate their needs at the expense of yours; similarly, do not overlook their needs and impose yours. The latter two approaches are short term and will most likely lead to further issues down the line.

Be mindful of your time (see **Strategy 8**). This can be a great source of stress and anxiety if not managed correctly. Time management and organisation are skills; which means that they can be learnt to your advantage.

Build healthy social interactions and a strong support network (see **Strategy 4**). During times of stress, a support network is essential. It can make the difference between successfully overcoming the stressful situation and becoming depressed.

Find your sense of purpose and good self-esteem (refer to **Strategy 1**). Purpose adds meaning to your life and decreases your mortality risk, according to a new study published in the journal *Psychological Science: (Purpose in Life as a Predictor of Mortality Across Adulthood, Hill PL, Turiano NA Psychol Sci 2014 May 8)*. The research suggests that having a purpose in life plays a unique role in promoting longevity regardless of age. Seek out your purpose – not only will it help you live longer; it will also allow you to look at the big picture. Big picture thinking puts things into perspective and allows you to distance yourself from the day-to-day stresses of life.

Nurture your sense of optimism and hope (refer to **Strategy 7**). Hope is a forgotten emotion, yet its power to captivate the imagination and allow you to feel a sense of happiness in the 'now' is understated. It is the positive version of anxiety.

Focus on building resilience (refer to **Strategy 6**). We all encounter tough times at some point in our lives. It is how we deal with it that sets the stage for the future. Bouncing back from tough times allows us to recover quickly from set-backs and focus on the things that are important in our lives and that make us happy. This is where resilience skills, play a huge role in our ability to move forward. The good news is that resilience skills can be learnt. **Strategy 6** provides an in-depth guide to developing resilience.

Spend time on things that you enjoy and have things to look forward to. Enjoyable activities are relaxing. They put things into perspective; reducing the levels of anxiety and stress you experience.

Therapy or Coaching are great stress relievers. In times of stress, I am a great believer in talking to someone who is a professional expert such as a therapist or coach. They can significantly help you raise your own self-awareness and empower you to regain control of your life. They work by guiding you towards an approach for managing stress and anxiety that works for you. They are also a huge source of emotional intelligence, providing you with the tools you need to move forward in difficult times.

In the UK, counselors and psychologists, registered either with the **UK Association of Counsellors and Psychotherapists (UKCP) (http://www.psychotherapy.org.uk/)**, **British Psychological Society (BPS) (http://www.bps.org.uk/**, **British Association of Counsellors and Psychotherapists (BACP) (http://www.bacp.co.uk/)** are recognised, qualified counsellors, psychotherapists and/or psychologists.

The **International Coach Federation (ICF) (http://www.coachfederation.org/)** is a global community of accredited coaches ranging from life coaching, executive coaching and leadership coaching.

Both coaching and therapy do not have to be expensive. Many of them offer subsidised services or group therapies which can be cost-effective.

In terms of proven therapies, **Cognitive Behavioural Therapy (CBT)** is an extremely cost-effective method that delivers results quickly. It works because it helps people to live in the present without dwelling on the past too much or worrying about the future. It prompts you to question the assumptions you have made about life and determine whether they are in fact, true. It promotes self-esteem and belief in yourself; and it teaches you to incorporate optimism in your life. It is most certainly a therapy to explore further whether in the form of a book or through a therapist or coach.

Prevention is better than cure. Invest in your well-being as a preventative measure – and you will save yourself a headache later on.

"An ounce of prevention is worth a pound of cure."

Benjamin Franklin, Founding Father of the United States (1706 – 1790)

"Health is a state of complete physical, mental and social well-being, and not merely the absence of disease or infirmity."

World Health Organization, 1948

Strategy 10: Leading

As we get older and progress through our careers or begin a family and become parents; the ability to lead becomes increasingly important. We find ourselves in a situation, where all of a sudden we are managing people either at work or at home; we are in a position of influence where what we say matters or has the power to persuade someone to take a particular action.

With this ability to lead and influence comes great responsibility. The impact we have on those we lead can be profound. As a result leadership can appear to be a scary task. People automatically assume that they do not have what it takes to lead and that one has to be born with leadership qualities. This is not the case. Leadership is a skill that can be learnt and everyone has the potential to become a great leader if nurtured in the right way. Not all of us have had the privileges of being exposed to 'role model' leaders or have received the training we need to become effective leaders. We just fall into it and eventually develop techniques that we find useful to help us manage and lead.

In fact, with social media, paving the way for so many members of the public to voice their opinions in ways that were never possible; it has created countless possibilities for people to emerge as leaders. The term 'following' as used by Twitter implies that you are in fact 'leading' people with your thoughts and ideas. Linked In uses the term 'influencing' and labels members as 'influencers'. Facebook allows you to emerge as a leader based on how many users like and/or comment on what you say.

With the right training and skills, we all have it within us to become excellent leaders. Based on my own experience, observations and leadership training, effective leadership starts from a position of trust. In fact, effective leadership is no different to the skills of influence, negotiation and persuasion that I mention in **Strategy 5**. Good leadership is the ability to influence somebody to act, behave or think in a specific way.

Leadership is influence.

John C. Maxwell, American Author, Speaker and Pastor

The key to successful leadership today is influence, not authority.

Kenneth Blanchard, American Author and Management Expert

There has been a significant amount of literature on styles and models of effective leadership over the years. The notion that good leadership was something that you were born with has been turned on its head since the 1950s; and there is now a lot more evidence to support the theory that leadership can be learnt. If we look at famous leaders: Nelson Mandela, Abraham Lincoln, Barack Obama, Mother Teresa, Mahatma Gandhi, Mao Zedong, Winston Churchill; none of them have similar personalities or are related. What they do have in common are the following strong leadership traits and qualities:

- Trustworthiness

- High Self-esteem and Confidence (See **Strategy 1**)

- Self-awareness (See **Strategy 4** and **Strategy 12**)

- Authenticity

- Honesty & Integrity

- Communication (See **Strategy 3**)

- Ability to Influence and Persuade (See **Strategy 5**)

- Ability to Delegate

- Creativity (See **Strategy 2**)

- Commitment

- Resilience (See **Strategy 6**)

- Collaborative

- Celebrate Success and Achievement (See **Strategy 11**)

In fact, if you have been able to master the other strategies, then you are on the leadership path.

Before you can influence, persuade or delegate to someone they need to be able to trust you. Trust can be tricky. Some people will trust you straight away, whereas others need more time. It cannot be rushed; and you cannot control how someone else views you. You can, however, control your own actions and behaviour; and in order to become more trustworthy you can be 'authentic': live by your values and be clear about who you are and what is important to you. Ensure your actions and behaviour reflects this. This creates a sense of stability – people know who you are and what to expect from you.

Once you have gained others' trust, they are more likely to listen to you and take your views on board. As explained in **Strategy 5**, influencing is a 'two-way' iterative process. You need to listen to the other person, understand their position as well as determine their values and needs in order to present your views in a way that resonates with them.

Values, needs and respect can be easily abused by leaders. If you want to be good leaders you need to value and respect those who you lead. By value and respect, I mean recognise good performance and celebrate the relevant person's success, give them your time, pay them fairly if you employ them, and actively seek their feedback and opinions on new initiatives. This raises their self-esteem and motivates them to perform better next time. It raises their profile and by association it raises your profile as the leader.

Outstanding leaders go out of their way to boost the self-esteem of their personnel. If people believe in themselves, it's amazing what they can accomplish.

Sam Walton, American Businessman and Entrepreneur (1918 – 1982)

"If you want to lift yourself up, lift up someone else."

Booker T. Washington, African American Educator, Author and Advisor to the Presidents of the United States (1856 – 1915)

"I've learned that people will forget what you said, people will forget what you did, but people will never forget how you made them feel. "

Maya Angelou, American Author and Poet (1928 – 2014)

Once you have been in a leadership position for a while, the challenge of maintaining the loyalty of your supporters, fans or employees kicks in. To maintain their loyalty, demonstrate your commitment, and perseverance to their causes, their growth and their development. Strive to understand their strengths and development areas so that you can help them achieve their full potential.

Actively create opportunities where they can apply their strengths as well as develop their weaknesses. This could simply be by delegating a task or involving them in a new project that facilitates this development. Give them something they have never done before. Challenge them, but let them know that you believe in their ability to do it and empower them to get the job done. Delegate.

Tell me and I will forget; teach me and I remember; involve me and I will learn."

Benjamin Franklin, Founding Father of the United States (1706 – 1790)

The growth and development of people is the highest calling of leadership.

Harvey Firestone, Father of the Firestone Tire and Rubber Company (1868 – 1938)

There is also an element of personal leadership that a good leader requires and that is, his own abilities to build resilience and cultivate creativity. Resilience is important because research has shown that the strongest of leaders have a natural ability to bounce back even in the worst of times. A long-standing reputation rests on the ability to navigate yourself away from crisis successfully. Leaders are role models for many people; when they have come out stronger from negative situations, they inspire hope in others.

Creativity is important because leaders need to be able to think out of the box when making decisions if the solutions presented to them are not appropriate.

Leadership is not a destination; it is a process and we are always growing and developing. There is no such thing as the perfect leader; there is such a thing as the authentic leader and this authenticity should shine through in everything you do.

Earn your leadership every day.

Michael Jordan, Former American Professional Basketball Player

Strategy 11: Practising Gratitude, Giving and Celebrating your Successes and Achievements

There are only two ways to live your life. One is as though nothing is a miracle. The other is as though everything is a miracle.

Albert Einstein, Physicist and Nobel Prize Winner (1879 – 1955)

Gratitude is a 'feel good' emotion. The more we have of it, the better we feel about ourselves. The better we feel, the more energised and motivated we are and the more likely we are to perform. The better we perform the more successful we are and the more successful we are, the more grateful we feel; resulting in a self-fulfilling cycle.

Sometimes we are caught up in the world around us and our daily challenges. We forget the wonderful aspects of our lives that make us happy. Human beings are naturally wired to focus on our negative challenges rather than focus on the things in our lives that are great and that we are lucky to have. This could be good friends, wonderful parents, education, the opportunity to travel the world, good health, a roof over our heads, food on the table or a wonderful talent. The list is endless.

Appreciating the good things is gratitude: the ability to consciously focus on the wonderful aspects of our lives; by shifting our perspective from the negative to the positive.

Practise gratitude

How do we actively detach from the negative and shift our focus to the positive? How do we cultivate an attitude of gratitude? The key, according to **Brother David Steindl-Rast**, a monk and interfaith scholar, is to view life as a series of moments. In each moment, observe the things in your life that you are grateful for. Practise mindfulness by only observing the beauty of the good things in your life. This will automatically shift your thinking to a positive place, allowing you to experience happiness in each moment.

Put your life in perspective and see the joy in all things. Look back at the times when you were happy or had achieved a goal in your life for which you are immensely grateful. Look at some of the events in your life that were life-changing; for example, when you met the love of your life, or you graduated from university, or the times when you met your closest friends; or an inspiring book that you read or a movie that you watched. Be grateful for these. Add them to a gratitude list.

Be thankful for the things in your present; your current job, your wonderful home, the food that you get to eat and experience every day, your health, your family, your friends, holidays, your skills and abilities. Add these to your gratitude list.

Next think about the opportunities you will have in the future or events to look forward to; this could be a job promotion, an opportunity to go back to education and pursue something you have always been passionate about, a holiday of a lifetime, meeting the love of your life, a medical treatment that will help you get better, anything at all that uplifts your spirits. The future affords you a choice of opportunities, which is exciting. It allows you to feel even more grateful. Put all of these on your gratitude list.

Read this gratitude list every morning. Try something different: read it aloud or sing it! You do not have to spend longer than 2 minutes on it. In fact, you could think about the list whilst brushing your teeth if you wanted to multi-task. It will help you start the day with the right mindset; and you will find that everything works out the way you want it to. Try it. You will be surprised at the results.

The other thing you can do is write thank you notes to people in your present, past or future, thanking them for something special they have done for you and how much it means to you. The writing of the 'thank you note' is a profound experience and once you have finished writing it, you will feel elated.

Gratitude is an easy and surefire way to increase the happiness in your life. Use it in every way you can and as often as you can. Write little 'Post-it' notes as reminders to practise gratitude; or add a calendar reminder. Embrace it into your daily routine.

"Let us rise up and be thankful, for if we didn't learn a lot today, at least we learned a little, and if we didn't learn a little, at least we didn't get sick, and if we got sick, at least we didn't die; so, let us all be thankful."

Buddha, Founded Buddhism (c.563-483 BC - c.483-411 BC)

"Opportunities, relationships, even money flowed my way when I learned to be grateful no matter what happened in my life."

Oprah Winfrey, Former American Talk Show Host and Philanthropist

"As we express our gratitude, we must never forget that the highest appreciation is not to utter words, but to live by them."

John F. Kennedy, 35th President of the United States (1917 – 1963)

Celebrate your successes and achievement

Keeping in tune with the theme of shifting the focus to positive things in our lives; one of the other things we do not do enough is give ourselves a pat on the back for the great things we have done. 'Great' does not have to be an amazing medical discovery or an award-winning movie production. It could simply be meeting a deadline at work; managing to get to the gym three times a week; being disciplined about eating healthily; being compliant with your medications; or giving that interview your best shot. All of these positive things should outweigh the negative things that we naturally tend to focus on.

Have little treats planned to reward yourself for meeting your goals; no matter how big or small these are. A sense of achievement leads to a sense of happiness and boosts your self-esteem. For your bigger goals, make sure you have a big celebration planned; it could be taking your friends and family out for dinner or going to a play you have always wanted to watch.

Celebrating your achievements is an important part of the happiness habit. If you do not celebrate your achievements you undervalue your abilities. Valuing your abilities is critical to your self-worth; a key factor in determining how happy you are.

Maintain a list of achievements; this will help you track all your achievements and can be a great motivational tool when you are feeling low or uncertain about how a certain task or event will play out. It also ensures that you acknowledge these and give them the recognition they deserve.

Do not forget to talk about your achievements. Tell people about them and let them acknowledge this. If you do not tell people, how will they know? This is not about 'blowing your own trumpet'; it is about promoting good work and recognising the hard work and effort you have put in to achieve something remarkable. You will find that your friends and family will be happy for you and proud; they will want to celebrate with you! People like to surround themselves around other people who are smart, successful and happy. This is another way to boost your happiness and self-esteem.

"The more you praise and celebrate your life, the more there is in life to celebrate."

Oprah Winfrey, Former American Talk Show Host and Philanthropist

Give back

Giving back creates a sense of nostalgia – a feeling of satisfaction that you have made a difference to someone's life or contributed to a cause in some way. It increases your sense of self-worth and in effect produces feelings of joy and reward.

It also allows you to feel 'needed'. From the time of our early ancestors, we all have an innate need to be relied upon; that our survival makes a difference to someone else's life. It motivates us in ways we have never thought about before.

It gives us perspective and lets us, view our lives differently relative to others, it invokes gratitude and brings out feelings of appreciation for the things that are present in our lives and absent in others.

Giving back does not necessarily have to be in the form of financial donations. It could be volunteering at your local charity or undertaking community service, visiting an elderly person at the local care home, cooking for an ill neighbor or helping a friend during a difficult time.

Community connections and networks are built this way. You may meet your best friend or the love of your life through this process; or somebody who makes a difference to your career and opens doors for you. There are opportunities in every connection.

Lastly, it allows us to grow and develop in new ways to build skills that we never had before. Invest your time and give back. When you look back at life, these are the things that make life worth living.

"The best way to find yourself is to lose yourself in the service of others."

Mahatma Gandhi, Preeminent Lader of Indian Nationalism in British-ruled India (1869 – 1948)

"Life is a gift, and it offers us the privilege, opportunity, and responsibility to give something back by becoming more."

Anthony Robbins, American Life Coach, Self-help Author and Motivational Speaker

"Only a life lived for others is a life worthwhile."

Albert Einstein, Physicist and Nobel Prize Winner (1879 – 1955)

Life is a gift. Be grateful for the past, present and the future yet to come. Celebrate your successes. Remember compliments. Give back to the world in some shape or form. It will compound your happiness and boost your mood. Life does not have to be perfect in order to experience a sense of happiness every day.

Strategy 12: The Strategy of Happiness

When I was 5 years old, my mother always told me that happiness was the key to life. When I went to school, they asked me what I wanted to be when I grew up. I wrote down 'happy'. They told me I didn't understand the assignment, and I told them they didn't understand life.

John Lennon, Emglish Musician, Singer and Founding Member of the Beatles (1940 -1980)

Happiness is a choice. However, when we struggle to make ends meet or face challenging or negative situations, we may question whether happiness is possible.

We will have difficult days. We will have days when someone makes us angry. We will have days when we let ourselves down. We will have days when things just do not go our way. We can, however, limit the impact the resulting negative emotions have on us. We can manage these days and move forward from them to a more hopeful and happier place.

By using the strategies in this book you can achieve and *maintain* a state of happiness. When good things happen, we learn to appreciate them and celebrate them. When we encounter negative things we learn to minimise their impact on how we feel and our behaviour.

Daniel Gilbert, Professor of Psychology at Harvard and author of the international bestseller, *Stumbling on Happiness* describes how humans have this ability to ponder the future and form images and thoughts of what might be. This can be a good thing or a bad thing. It is a good thing, when we visualise a happy and promising future; when we are hopeful. However, when we visualise a negative future, we become anxious. This anxiety prevents us from being happy even though it is not real and is an imagined state in the future. When the actual event does occur, it is very different to what we imagined it to be. In that moment, we are actually able to deal with it and we learn to be happy again.

This suggests that in the present, we are 'accepting' of our positions and learn to be happy with whatever situation we are in. He calls this 'synthetic happiness' rather than 'natural happiness'. He uses the example of somebody who wins the lottery compared to somebody who becomes paraplegic and what their states of mind are after one year. He found that a paraplegic person has the same level of happiness as the person who won the lottery. The reason for this is that our 'psychological immune system' protects and helps us to heal and be happy again, in spite of negative events. Synthetic happiness may appear to be inferior to natural happiness; however, we experience the same state of happiness regardless of what situation we are in; we can be happy if we employ the right strategies and mindset.

Martin Seligman, a former president of the American Psychological Association and author of various self-help books has pioneered this idea of positive psychology. He promotes the idea of nurturing a healthy mental well-being rather than just focusing on negative states of mind and mental health disorders. His theories build on the principles of cognitive behavioural therapy (CBT) which aims to transform unhelpful thinking patterns, feelings and behaviour into healthier ways of functioning.

He strongly believes that leading an 'engaged' and 'meaningful' life helps achieve a happy state. When 'engaged' or engrossed in what we are doing, we have no time to experience negative thoughts. A 'meaningful' life is one where we have a 'sense of purpose' (refer to **Strategy 1**) and where we identify environments which allow us to carry out this sense of purpose, allow our strengths and values to thrive and are surrounded by communities who support us.

He also promotes the idea of a 'Gratitude visit' where you go back in time to a place where you have been 'enormously thankful' to someone. This builds up positive feelings of happiness and puts you in the state of happiness.

For relationships, he prescribes that couples should identify an activity they both enjoy and/are good at and design a day or evening a week where they get to participate in this activity. The idea is that when the couple participate in an activity together that they both enjoy or are good at, it boosts their individual self-esteem and strengthens the relationship.

Practicing activities that put you in a happy state of mind is extremely important; a happy state of mind allows you to consistently perform well at work and remain motivated. (Remember, success is 80% how you feel and 20% skill.)

This then becomes a habit and you start to live in this state. It becomes a self-fulfilling prophesy.

Remember:

50% of happiness is genetic; the other 50% is in your control. Your thoughts, feelings and actions can significantly influence your happiness which are all in your control.

Relationships are the key to happiness. Nurture your existing relationships, expand your network, and grow your connections. It will be a worthwhile investment.

Experiences leave a stronger emotional footprint than tangible goods, whose effects on happiness are short-term. Experiences lead to memories which we can reminisce and which bring about positive effects on long-term happiness.

Money does not necessarily buy you happiness. Those who win the lottery are no happier than the average person. (The only exception to this is if you are either giving back to charity or the community or if you have significantly raised your social status as a result of increased wealth.)

I wish you all the happiness and success in the world. Never stop believing in yourself and always be true to yourself. You are worth more than you think. Continue to develop mentally, physically and emotionally. Never stop learning. **Never stop investing in your own happiness and success.**

Happiness is not something ready made. It comes from your own actions.

Dalai Lama, formerly known as Tenzin Gyatso, 14th Dalai Lama and Spiritual and Temporal Leader of Tibet

Made in the USA
Lexington, KY
24 January 2015